Knowing
Beyond Words

REFLECTIONS ON THE INEXPRESSIBLE

John McQuiston II

MOREHOUSE PUBLISHING
Harrisburg, Pennsylvania

Copyright © 2002 John McQuiston II

Morehouse Publishing
P.O. Box 1321
Harrisburg, PA 17105

Morehouse Publishing is a division of The Morehouse Group.

We have made every effort to trace and identify sources correctly and to secure the necessary permission for printing. If we have made any errors in this text, we apologize sincerely. Please notify Morehouse Publishing if any corrections are to be made in subsequent printings.

The Scripture quotations, unless otherwise specified, are from the *Book of Common Prayer* (1662) and The King James Version of the Bible. Where noted, quotations are from the New Revised Standard Version (NRSV) © 1994 or the Revised Standard Version (RSV) © 1973 and are used with permission.

Cover design: Trude Brummer.

Library of Congress Cataloging-in-Publication Data

McQuiston, John.
    Knowing beyond words : reflections on the inexpressible /
John McQuiston II
        p. cm.
    Includes bibliographical references.
    ISBN 0-8192-1901-0
    1. Spiritual Life—Quotations, maxims, etc. I. Title.

BL624.M3987 2002
291.4'32—dc21   2001042800

Printed in the United States of America

02 03 04 05 06 07 08 09   9 8 7 6 5 4 3 2 1

Uttering a word is like striking a note on the keyboard of imagination.

Ludwig Wittgenstein
Philosophical Investigations

Contents

Introduction

God employs many translators.
—John Donne

In the religious sphere, the danger of forgetting that our words are merely man-made symbols is acute. Paul Tillich warned of the "sin of religion:" the worship of one's religion. Too frequently we become so attached to our ways of thinking and speaking that we forget that they are only creations of the human mind. We not only forget that our forms of worship are designed by man, but also that our ideas about the nature of the world spring from our own thoughts. As contemporary physicist Roger S. Jones says: "Since experiences cannot be divorced from consciousness, our perceptions amount to mental constructs or representations. When we treat these representations as reality, we commit a profound idolatry."[1]

To help us avoid the error of confusing our religious symbols, however profound, with reality, we should remind ourselves that there are many ways of thinking and speaking. As theologian Abraham Heschel says: "God's voice speaks in many languages, communicating itself in a diversity of intuitions. The word of God never comes to an end. No word is God's last word."[2]

One of the most elegant expressions of religious thought is found in the 1662 version of the Anglican *Book of Common Prayer*. It is the starting place this exploration, these attempts to speak of God, death, joy, meaning, and other critical, but ultimately indefinable, matters.

The 1662 version of the *Book of Common Prayer* is a classic that has survived the test of time. The versions of the *Book of Common Prayer* in current use, and there are many of them, trace their origin to Thomas Cranmer's original prayer book. In turn, it was an adaptation of Roman Catholic services that had evolved over many centuries. The earliest roots of those Roman Catholic liturgies can be traced to Jewish sources thousands of years old.

The *Book of Common Prayer* is filled with traditional images that are today revered by many and rejected by many. *Knowing*

Beyond Words is an effort to rediscover the spirit behind the traditional images by juxtaposing passages from the 1662 work with contrasting and complementary expressions from literary, religious, and even scientific sources. These illustrate theologian Panikkar's insight that "truth is pluralistic because reality itself is pluralistic, not being an objectifiable entity. We are not only spectators of the Real, we are also co-actors and even co-authors of it. This is precisely our human dignity."[3]

Whatever words and images are used, ultimately it is their underlying spirit we seek, because, as Paul said in his letter to the Corinthians, literalism destroys the very truth it attempts to speak (2 Cor. 3:6).

Almighty God, bestow upon us the meaning of words, the light of understanding, the nobility of diction and the faith of the true nature. And grant that what we believe we may also speak.
    —St. Hilary

1. Attempts to Speak of the Nature of God

In 1886 Friedrich Nietzsche wrote: "The greatest event of recent times—that God is dead, that the belief in the Christian God is no longer tenable—is beginning to cast its first shadows over Europe."[4] But is God dead? Or is it merely that the traditional Western image of God as an "old man in the sky" is dead?

Is any image of God, or of Reality "true"? W. MacNeile Dixon writes: "The theologians of all ages and races have formed an image of God after their own fancies, and nothing could be more improbable than that He represents in the least particular their conception."[5] This is not a new insight. The biblical commandment against idolatry tells us we fall into error anytime we accept anything made by humans as divine.

Still, we have no choice but to think of God using mental constructs. We seek images that are not only familiar to us, but also that create meaning and connection. Even as we remind ourselves of the symbolic nature of our words and ideas, we cannot help but continue the search for more authentic ways to think and communicate. Although we may admit that we will never find *the* truth, and despite the knowledge that any image, any name, and any idea of "God" must ultimately fail, we still continue to look for better metaphors for the Incomprehensible Reality "in whom we live and move and have our being" (Acts 17:28). Our need is personal, even if we do not imagine God as depicted by Michelangelo on the ceiling of the Sistine Chapel. If we no longer think of God as "out there" or "up there," we may look "within us" or "between us."

I believe in God the Father Almighty
Maker of heaven and earth.

> Apostles' Creed

My religion consists of a humble admiration of the illimitable superior spirit who reveals himself in the slight details we are able to perceive with our frail and feeble minds. That deeply emotional conviction of the presence of a superior reasoning power, which is revealed in the incomprehensible universe, forms my idea of God.

> Albert Einstein
> Quoted in his *New York Times* obituary
> 19 April 1955

If I answer, I worship what I know, they immediately reply, What is the essence of the object of worship? Then, if I confess that I am ignorant of the essence, they turn on me again and say, So you worship you know not what.

St. Basil the Great
Epistle CCXXXIV

The closest we can come to thinking about God is as a process rather than a being.

David Cooper
God Is a Verb

The secret of God in the universe: God is shapeless, colorless, without similarity. Whatever form or condition mankind sees, it is not God.

> Ali Shariati
> *Haji*

If any one, having seen God, understood what he saw, he did not see *Him*.

Dionysius the Areopagite
Letter to Gaius Therapeutes

God is the creating spirit that calls order out of chaos. God is the life force that emerges first into consciousness, then into self-consciousness, and now into self-transcendence, and ultimately into we know not what. God is the love that creates wholeness, the Being at the depths of our being, the Source from which all life comes.

John Shelby Spong
Resurrection

God is not considered as Being, as Substance, as the more or less transcendent Absolute, but as "genitival" Relationship . . . the Reality *of* Reality, the Truth *of* Truth. God is a reality so "real" as not even to be capable of being thought as existing externally or independently of the things for which God is precisely God . . . ultimately God is not a "thing," not even the sublimest of things . . . God is pure relationship . . .

Raimundo Panikkar
The Silence of God

God is not to be treated as an exception to all metaphysical principles, invoked to save their collapse. He is their chief exemplification.

Alfred North Whitehead
Process and Reality

God is the poet of the world, with tender patience leading it by his vision of truth, beauty and goodness.

Alfred North Whitehead
Process and Reality

It would be a great victory for Christian apologetics if the words "God" and "existence" were very definitely separated except in the paradox of God becoming manifest under the conditions of existence. God does not exist. He is being itself, beyond essence and existence. Therefore to argue that God exists is to deny him.

> Paul Tillich
> *Systematic Theology*

There is no God external to life. God, rather, is the inescapable depth and center of all that is. God is not a being superior to all other beings. God is the Ground of Being.

John Shelby Spong
Why Christianity Must Change or Die

The Tao that can be spoken is not the Eternal Tao.
The name that can be named is not the Eternal name.
The Nameless is the origin of heaven and earth.

Tao Te Ching

At the deepest levels of divinity, all opposites and distinctions vanish, overwhelmed by oneness.

Daniel Matt
The Essential Kabbalah

I am heat and light; I give and withhold the rain.
I am immortality and I am death;
I am what is and what is not.

The Bhagavad Gita

God said unto Moses:
"I am that I am."

Exodus 3:14

Thou art That.

Chandogya Upanishad

Rabbi Menachem Nahum of Chernobyl [said] "All being itself is derived from God and the presence of the Creator is in each created thing." This double notion is pan-entheism. Pan-entheism, according to David Tracy, theologian at the University of Chicago, is the private view of most Christian intellectuals today. Not only is God immanent in everything, as plain old pantheists hold, however loosely, but more profoundly everything is simultaneously in God, within God the transcendent.

Annie Dillard
"Holy Sparks: A Prayer for the Silent God"

The second commandment implies more than the prohibition of images; it implies rejection of all visible symbols for God; not only images fashioned by man but also of "any manner of likeness, of any thing that is in heaven above, or that is in the earth beneath, or that is in the water under the earth.". . . And yet there is something in the world that the Bible does regard as a symbol of God. It is not a temple or a tree, it is not a statue or a star. The symbol of God is man, every man. God created man in His image, in His likeness.

Abraham Joshua Heschel
Man's Quest for God

When the western world accepted Christianity, Caesar conquered. The brief Galilean vision of humility flickered through the ages uncertainly. The deeper idolatry, of the fashioning of God in the image of Egyptian, Persian, and Roman imposed rulers, was retained. The church gave unto God the attributes which belonged exclusively to Caesar.

Alfred North Whitehead
Process and Reality

Anything visible, and anything that can be grasped by thought is bounded. Anything bounded is finite. Anything finite is not undifferentiated. Conversely the boundless is called *Ein Sof,* Infinite. It is absolute undifferentiation in perfect changeless oneness. Since it is boundless, there is nothing outside of it. Since it transcends and conceals itself, it is the essence of everything hidden and revealed.

Daniel Matt
The Essential Kabbalah

In the beginning was God,
Today is God,
Tomorrow will be God,
Who can make an image of God?
He has no body.
He is a word which comes out of your mouth.
That word! It is no more,
It is past, and it still lives!
So is God.

> John S. Mbiti
> from *The Prayers of African Religion*

Arouse yourself to contemplate, to focus thought, for God is the annihilation of all thoughts, uncontainable by any concept. Indeed, since no one can contain God at all, it is called Nothingness, *Ayin*.

Daniel Matt
The Essential Kabbalah

Man has always sought something beyond all this pain, anxiety, and sorrow. Is there something that is sacred, eternal, that is beyond all the reaches of thought? This has been a question from the most ancient of times. What is it that is sacred? What is that which has no time, that which is incorruptible, that which is nameless, that which has no quality, no limitation, the timeless, the eternal? Is there such a thing? Man has asked this for thousands and thousands of years. So he has worshipped the sun, the earth, nature, the trees, the birds; everything that is living on this earth man has worshipped since ancient times. The *Vedas* and the *Upanishads* never mention God. That which is supreme, they said, is not manifested.

> J. Krishnamurti
> *Total Freedom*

The concept of "God" is not a grasp of God by which a person masters the mystery, but it is letting oneself be grasped by the mystery which is present yet ever distant.

Karl Rahner
Foundations of Christian Faith

O Hidden Life, vibrant in every atom,
O Hidden Light, shining in every creature,
O Hidden Love, embracing all in Oneness,
May each who feels himself as one with Thee
Know he is therefore one with every other.

Annie Besant
The Oxford Book of Prayer

The most noble of the truths is silence.

Candrakirti
Prasannapada

Thou art inexpressible, ineffable, and only with silence canst thou be embraced.

Hermes Trismegistus

Then the LORD answered Job
  out of the whirlwind:
"Who is this that darkens counsel by
words without knowledge?"

Job 38:1-2 (RSV)

I know only enough of God to want to worship him, by any means ready to hand. There is an anomalous specificity to all our experience in space, a scandal of particularity, by which God burgeons up or showers down into the shabbiest of occasions, and leaves his creation's dealings with him in the hands of purblind and clumsy amateurs.

Annie Dillard
Holy the Firm

To speak *of* God, even for the purpose of denying God's existence, is to "transform" God into the order of creatures, and so is tantamount to destroying God.

Raimundo Panikkar
The Silence of God

About that which one cannot speak, one must remain silent.

Ludwig Wittgenstein and Bertrand Russell
Tractatus Logico-philosophicus

God is love;
And he that dwelleth in love
Dwelleth in God,
And God in him.

1 John 4:16

God spake these words, and said:
I am the Lord thy God . . .
Thou shalt have none other gods but me.
Thou shalt not make to thyself any graven image,
Nor the likeness of anything that is in heaven above,
Or in the earth beneath, or in the water under the earth.
Thou shalt not bow down to them, nor worship them.

First and Second Commandments
Book of Common Prayer

2. Attempts to Speak of Creating Joy

Many prayer books and hymns exhort us to be thankful to God and to love God. But surely God does not need our thanks or our love. Why then is there such an emphasis on love and gratitude? The answer may be that it is we who need to be thankful and loving, not because we owe it to God, but because by consciously adopting these attitudes, we change ourselves. For most of us, stopping to think of things for which we are thankful corrects our perspective and improves our quality of life. When we are thankful, it is difficult to be bitter and disappointed. When we perform acts of loving kindness, we discover the joy of focusing on others, and our own concerns become less significant. If we change ourselves, we change the world in which we live, and increase not only our own joy and satisfaction, but that of others.

O go your way into his gates with thanksgiving,
And into his courts with praise:
Be thankful unto him,
And speak good of his Name.
For the Lord is gracious,
His mercy is everlasting:
And his truth endureth from generation to generation.

Psalm 100
Book of Common Prayer

It is very meet, right, and our bounden duty,
That we should at all times, and in all places,
Give thanks unto thee, O Lord.

> Communion Service
> *Book of Common Prayer*

Thou shalt love the Lord thy God,
With all thy heart,
And with all thy soul,
And with all thy mind.
This is the first
And great commandment.
And the second is like unto it,
Thou shalt love thy neighbour as thyself.

Matthew 22:37-39

My religion is kindness.

Attributed to the Dalai Lama

As a man thinketh in his heart, so is he.

Adapted from Proverbs 23:7

You are the music while the music lasts.

T. S. Eliot
Four Quartets

Our life is shaped by our mind, we become what we think.

The Dhammapada

For whatsoever a man soweth,
That also shall he reap.

Galatians 6:7

Paradise has never been lost and therefore is never regained. As Staretz Zosima says, according to Father Merton, as soon as one wishes for it, that is to say, as soon as I become conscious of the fact, paradise is right away with me, and the experience is the foundation on which the kingdom of heaven is built. Eschatology is something never realizable and yet realized at every moment in our life. We see it always ahead of us though we are in reality always in it. This is the delusion we are conditioned to have as beings in time or rather "becomings" in time. This delusion ceases to be one the very moment we experience all this. It is the Great Mystery, intellectually speaking. In Christian terms, it is the Divine Wisdom.

D. T. Suzuki
In Merton, *Zen and the Birds of Appetite*

This man is freed from servile bands, of hope to rise, or fear
   to fall;
Lord of himself, though not of lands, and having nothing,
   yet hath all.

   Sir Henry Wotton
   The Character of a Happy Life (1614)

If one does not understand by eternity the endless duration of time but rather timelessness, then he who loves in the present lives eternally.

Ludwig Wittgenstein and Bertrand Russell
Tractus Logico-philosophicus

I thank You God
for most this amazing day.

> e. e. cummings
> *three poems*

One of the holiest women I have ever known did little with her life in terms of worldly success; her gift was that of bringing laughter with her wherever she went. No matter how dark or grievous the occasion, wherever she was, Holy laughter was present to heal and redeem. In the Koran it is written, "He deserves Paradise who makes his companions laugh."

Madeleine L'Engle
Walking on Water

All that is comes from the mind; it is based upon the mind; it is fashioned by the mind. For hatred does not cease by hatred, hatred ceases by love. This is the eternal law.

The Dhammapada

The Kingdom of God
Is within you.

Luke 17:21

The world of the happy individual is a different one from that of the unhappy individual.

Ludwig Wittgenstein and Bertrand Russell
Tractatus Logico-philosophicus

Life carries all things away and you crave for stability and permanence. So you fear life and you fear death because you cling. When you cling to nothing, when you have no fear of losing anything, then you are free to flow like the mountain stream that is always fresh and sparkling and alive.

Anthony De Mello
The Way to Love

Time is not there for us to build a society but rather to "enjoy." The ideal, mystical life might be one lived in, to put it awkwardly, a succession of what Elie Wiesel would call "eternal moments." An example that Panikkar gives us of what we might call "other-worldly time" is seen in the life of certain monks for whom all hurry loses its meaning. Efficiency and purpose fade away. The person living this way *is*, not *does* or *has*.

Harry James Cargas
Introduction to *Invisible Harmony*

There is no fear in love,
But perfect love casteth out fear.

1 John 4:18

Him I call a Brahmin who fears neither prison nor death.
He has the power of love no army can defeat.

The Dhammapada

He who sees Me in all, and sees all in Me, for him I am not lost, and he is not lost for Me.

Bhagavad Gita

In Whitehead Western metaphysics moved closer than ever before to formulating the content of the ancient saying "God is love." What is the root idea of love but this, participation by one subject in the life of others. If value is found in participating, in living the life of another, then supreme value must be the supreme form of such integration of the many into the one. Then there can be no final stage, only an inexhaustible progress of the divine life.

Charles Hartshorne
Whitehead's Philosophy: Selected Essays, 1935–1970

For, behold, I create new heaven and a new earth.

Isaiah 65:17

And I saw a new heaven and a new earth:
For the first heaven and the first earth were passed away.
And I John saw the holy city, New Jerusalem,
Coming down from God out of heaven.

Revelation 21:1-2

If you do not change now, you will never change. Transformation can only take place immediately; the revolution is now, not tomorrow. When that happens, you are completely without a problem, for then the self is not worried about itself; then you are beyond the wave of destruction.

J. Krishnamurti
Total Freedom

We are not an audience watching the God-ing process on stage. We are on stage, ourselves. Nothing is inconsequential . . . Every encounter with another being is a point of contact on which the universe pivots.

David Cooper
God Is a Verb

If I see blue or white, the seeing of my eyes is identical with what is seen. The eye by which I see God is the same as the eye by which God sees me. My eye and God's eye are one and the same.

Meister Eckhart

You are my witnesses says the Lord.

Isaiah 43:10 (RSV)

The meaning of human life no longer lies in the historical fulfillment of a mission but in the realization of the human being . . . the *today* of the Easter liturgy in the Christian rite. Today the world is redeemed, because today it is created and today risen again. . . . We create time . . . It is our child. The only reality is the creative instant . . . Paradise is the today . . . The meaning of life is not tomorrow, but today.

Raimundo Panikkar
Cosmotheandric Experience

If ye then
Be risen with Christ,
Seek those things which are above,
Where Christ sitteth
On the right hand of God.
Set your affection
On things above,
Not on things on the earth.

Colossians 3:1

Thou shalt shew me the path of life;
In thy presence is the fulness of joy:
And at thy right hand
There is pleasure for evermore.

Psalm 16:12
Book of Common Prayer

Come, Holy Ghost, our souls inspire,
And lighten with celestial fire
Thou the anointing Spirit art,
Who dost thy seven-fold gifts impart.
Thy blessed Unction from above
Is comfort, life, and fire of love.

Ordering of Priests, *Veni, Creator Spiritus*
Book of Common Prayer

Almighty God, Father of all mercies,
We thine unworthy servants
Do give thee most humble and hearty thanks
For all thy goodness and loving-kindness
To us and to all men;
We bless thee for our creation,
Preservation, and all the blessings of this life;
But above all for thine inestimable love
In the redemption of the world
By our Lord Jesus Christ,
For the means of grace,
And for the hope of glory.
And we beseech thee,
Give us that due sense of all thy mercies,
That our hearts may be unfeignedly thankful.

General Thanksgiving
Book of Common Prayer

3. Attempts to Speak of the Search for Meaning

◦◦

What is the meaning of life? Why do we exist? Is there a purpose? For millennia we have asked these questions, and composed a variety of responses. The responses we give—in sacred literature, in myths, folktales, and in scholarly journals— reveal both our most basic beliefs and the limits of our knowledge. Each of us lives a theology, even if it is unconscious. We desire to live a meaningful life. We want meaningful work. To live without meaning in life leads to hopelessness and depression. So each of us seeks meaning in his or her own way, whether in a science laboratory or in acts of kindness, whether in abstract philosophical reasoning or in caring for family and friends, whether looking through a telescope or looking for a cause.

. . . As the hart desireth the water-brooks:
So longeth my soul after thee, O God.
My soul is athirst for God,
Yea, even for the living God:
When shall I come to appear before the presence of God?

Psalm 42:1-2
Book of Common Prayer

O God, thou art my God: early will I seek thee.
My soul thirsteth for thee, my flesh also longeth after thee:
In a barren and dry land where no water is.
Thus have I looked for thee in holiness:
That I might behold thy power and glory.
For thy loving-kindness is better than the life itself:
My lips shall praise thee.

> Psalm 63:1-4
> *Book of Common Prayer*

One thing I have learned in a long life: that all our science, measured against reality, is primitive and childlike.

Albert Einstein
Albert Einstein: Creator and Rebel

One could argue that the affirmation of God's existence is the result of a desire to comprehend reality in all its mystery.

Anthony M. Matteo
"Can Belief in God Be Basic?"

No longer does one do as God wills, set over against some imaginary creature in heaven. Rather, in one's own person he tries to achieve what the creative powers of Emergent Being have themselves so far achieved in lower forms of life. The problem of meaningless is the form in which nonbeing poses itself in our time; then, says Tillich, the task of conscious beings at the height of their evolutionary destiny is to meet and vanquish this new emergent obstacle to sentient life.

Ernest Becker
The Denial of Death

The human mind is a faculty in search of its intuition, that is, of assimilation with being, with pure and simple being, supremely one, without distinction as to essence and existence or possibility or actuality.

Joseph Marechal
Etudes sur le psycologie de mystiques I

The meaning of the world must lie outside of it.

Ludwig Wittgenstein and Bertrand Russell
Tractatus Logico-philosophicus

We don't usually think of what we see as an image at all but simply as a tree. We are, for the most part, unconscious that light is entering our eyes and forming a pattern on the retina, and that this pattern of visual sensations must be interpreted by the mind . . . We are unconscious of our own figuration . . . The categorization and naming of different objects, which underlies the paradoxes of set theory, also conceals the basic assumption that the world consists of distinct divisible things. Our very thought processes and language reflect the illusion of separateness and disunity. The fundamental analytic method of science is at stake here. Can cause and effect, mind and matter, subject and object ever really be treated as separate and discrete? For the resolution (or is it dissolution?) of these dilemmas, I look to the renunciation of idolatry and the unification of science and the humanities.

Roger S. Jones
Physics as Metaphor

To reach this essential union of love of God, a person must be careful not to lean on imaginative visions, forms, figures or particular ideas, since they cannot serve as a proportionate and proximate means for such an effect; they would be a hindrance instead.

St. John of the Cross
Ascent of Mt. Carmel

And if any man think that he knoweth anything,
He knoweth nothing yet as he ought to know.

1 Corinthians 8:2

If one believes one knows, one does not know.

Kena Upanishad

So thought constructs a verbal or nonverbal structure of God, otherness, immensity, timelessness, and so on. But it is still the product of thought so it is still material . . . can the mind be free of form? Words make it so difficult. Words are necessary in order to communicate, but if you live merely at the verbal level they are absolutely useless.

J. Krishnamurti
Total Freedom

Finally, there is deity, which is that factor in the universe whereby there is importance, value, and ideal beyond the actual. There must be value beyond ourselves. Otherwise everything experienced would be merely a barren detail on our own solipsist mode of existence.

Alfred North Whitehead
Modes of Thought

So what we call scientific knowledge today is a body of statements of varying degrees of certainty. Some of them are most unsure; some of them are nearly sure; but none is absolutely certain. Scientists are used to this. We know that it is consistent to be able to live and not know . . . What, then, is the meaning of it all? What can we say today to dispel the mystery of existence? If we take everything into account, not only what the ancients knew, but also all those things that we have found out up to today that they didn't know, then I think we must frankly admit that we do not know.

Richard P. Feynman
The Meaning of It All

Such knowledge is too wonderful and excellent for me:
I cannot attain unto it.
Whither shall I go then from thy Spirit:
Or whither shall I go then from thy presence?

Psalm 139:5
Book of Common Prayer

4. Attempts to Speak of Giving

The cynic observes that the emphasis religious leaders place on giving is manipulative. We have all observed situations where this has been so. But most pleas for help are sincere. We feel compelled to give aid and assistance. What lies behind our need to respond to the needs of others?

We think of giving as something done for the benefit of the recipient. And while that is true, every faith tradition teaches that giving is necessary for the spiritual health of the giver. Giving reduces our self-absorption. By giving, we discover the joy of helping others. Through giving, we learn that what is truly valuable is not material. We free ourselves, at least in part, from dependence upon our possessions. We remind ourselves that our real security and self worth does not come from the amount of money in our bank accounts.

To do good and to distribute forget not;
For with such sacrifices God is well pleased.

Communion Service
Book of Common Prayer

The Lord is my shepherd:
therefore can I lack nothing.

Psalm 23:1
Book of Common Prayer

Ye cannot serve God and Mammon.
Therefore I say unto you,
Take no thought for your life,
What ye shall eat or what ye shall drink;
Nor yet for your body, what ye shall put on.
Is not the life more than meat, and the body more
    than raiment?

Matthew 6:24-25

Be ye doers of the word,
And not hearers only,
Deceiving your own selves.
Pure religion and undefiled before God and the Father is this,
To visit the fatherless
And widows in their affliction.

James 1:22, 27

Loss of self or loss of material things, which is worse?
Those who are attached to things will suffer,
those who are contented are never disappointed,
they endure forever.

Tao Te Ching

For what will it profit a man
If he gains the whole world
And forfeits his life?

Matthew 16:26 (RSV)

You have the right to work, but never to the fruit of work. You should never engage in action for the sake of reward, nor should you long for inaction. Perform work in this world, Arjuna, as a man established within himself—without selfish attachments, and alike in success and defeat. For yoga is perfect evenness of mind. Seek refuge in the attitude of detachment and you will amass the wealth of spiritual awareness. Those who are motivated only by desire for the fruits of action are miserable, for they are constantly anxious about the results of what they do.

Bhagavad Gita

Every world religion, no matter what its philosophical view, is founded first and foremost on the precept that we must reduce our selfishness and serve others.

The Dalai Lama
The Wisdom Teachings of the Dalai Lama

How should man, a being created in the likeness of God, live? What way of living is compatible with the grandeur and mystery of living? It is a problem which man has always been anxious to ignore.

Abraham Joshua Heschel
God in Search of Man

In what dimension of existence does man become aware
of the grandeur and earnestness of living? What are the
occasions in which he discovers the nature of his own self?

Abraham Joshua Heschel
God in Search of Man

It is in the employment of his will, not in reflection, that he meets his own self as it is; not as he should like it to be. In his deeds man exposes his immanent as well as his suppressed desires, spelling even that which he cannot apprehend. What he may not dare to think, he often utters in deeds. The heart is revealed in the deeds.

Abraham Joshua Heschel
God in Search of Man

If I spend my life wanting what I do not have, I will spend my life in hell. If I spend my life loving what I have been given, I will spend my life in heaven. Grant me the grace and strength to love what I have.

Rabi'a al-'Adawiya (d. A.D. 80)

The whole secret of spiritual transformation is turning selfish desire into selfless desire, transforming personal passions into the overwhelming desire to attain life's highest goal.

Eknath Easwaren
Dialogue with Death

This is the first and great commandment:

Love the Lord your God
With all your heart, and with all your soul,
And with all your mind.
The second is like unto it:
Love your neighbor as yourself.
On these two commandments
Hang all the law and the prophets.

Matthew 22:37-40 (NRSV)

The important thing is not to think much but to love much.

Teresa of Avila

Lord, make me an instrument of peace,
Where there is hatred, let me sow love,
Where there is injury, pardon,
Where there is doubt, faith,
Where there is despair, hope,
Where there is darkness, light,
Where there is sadness, joy.

O divine Master, grant that I may not so much seek
To be consoled as to console,
To be understood as to understand,
To be loved as to love.

For it is in giving that we receive,
It is in forgiving that we are forgiven,
It is in dying to self that we are born to ultimate life.

Francis of Assisi

Inner tranquillity comes from the development of love and compassion. The more we care for the happiness of others, the greater is our own sense of well-being. Cultivating a close, warmhearted feeling for others automatically puts the mind at ease and opens our inner door. It helps remove whatever fears or insecurities we may have and gives us the strength to cope with any obstacles we encounter.

The Dalai Lama
The Wisdom Teachings of the Dalai Lama

The words "experience of love" must not be understood in terms of emotional fulfillment, of desire and possession, but of full realization, total awakening—a complete realization of love not merely as the emotion of a feeling but as the wide openness of Being itself, the realization that Pure Being is Infinite Giving or that Absolute Emptiness is Absolute Compassion. This realization is not intellectual, not abstract, but concrete. It is, in Christ's words, "Spirit and Life."

Thomas Merton
Zen and the Birds of Appetite

And we most humbly beseech thee,
O heavenly Father,
So to assist us with thy grace,
That we may continue in that holy fellowship,
And do all such good works
As thou hast prepared for us to walk in.

Book of Common Prayer

Only one who has enough is truly rich.

Tao Te Ching

Thou shalt not covet thy neighbour's house,
Thou shalt not covet thy neighbour's wife,
Nor his manservant, nor his maidservant,
Nor his ox, nor his ass,
Nor anything that is thy neighbour's.

Exodus 20:17

Grant, we beseech thee, Almighty God,
That the words that we have heard this day with our
    outward ears,
May through thy grace be so grafted inwardly in our hearts,
That they may bring forth in us the fruit of good living.

A Post Communion Prayer
Book of Common Prayer

But godliness with contentment is great gain.
For we brought nothing into this world,
And it is certain we can carry nothing out.

1 Timothy 6:6-7

5. Attempts to Speak of Prayer and Meditation

When we pray and when we meditate we do many things at once. Physically, we lower our blood pressure. Emotionally, we increase our satisfaction with life. If we meditate regularly, we are told, we reduce the risk of disease and extend our life span. Spiritually, we address ourselves to the Infinite: we seek a profound link with God, the Ultimate, the source of All.

There are many ways to pray, some with words, some in silence. In the rush of time, our time, we address God, however we understand God, the Eternal, the Mystery of existence. We seek detachment from daily duties, from commerce. For a time we may share in what is timeless.

Almighty God, unto whom all hearts be open,
All desires known, and from whom no secrets are hid:
Cleanse the thoughts of our hearts
By the inspiration of thy Holy Spirit,
That we may perfectly love thee,
And worthily magnify thy holy Name;
Through Christ our Lord.

Book of Common Prayer

To conquer yourself for your own good is to make use of the senses to serve the interior life. If you are praying, you must remember that there is One within you to Whom you can pray; if you are listening, you can listen to Him Who is nearer to you than anyone else. If you like, you never need to withdraw from this good companionship.

Teresa of Avila
The Way of Perfection

Prayer is not us trying to grab hold of God. Prayer is to recognize God coming to us.

Stephen Verney

Genuine prayer is an event in which man surpasses himself. Man hardly comprehends what is coming to pass. Its beginning lies on this side of the word, but the end lies beyond all words.

Abraham Joseph Heschel
Man's Quest for God

St. Augustine says: "Pour out, that you may be filled, learn not to love this that you may love that. Turn away from thence that you may turn thither." Plainly he means that to accept or receive you must be empty.

Meister Eckhart

Each day the student of learning seeks new knowledge,
each day the student of the Tao drops something more.
By continued dispossession one reaches doing no thing,
by leaving everything undone, everything is done.
The world of things is conquered by doing nothing.

Tao Te Ching

The only real rest comes when you are alone with God.

Rumi
The Essential Rumi

[Those who wish to meditate should] learn to remain in God's presence with a loving attention and a tranquil intellect. For little by little the divine calm and peace with a wondrous sublime knowledge of God, enveloped in divine love, will be infused in their souls. They should not interfere with imaginings. Otherwise the soul will be disquieted and drawn out of its peaceful contentment. And if scruples about their inactivity arise, they should remember that pacification of the soul (making it calm and peaceful, inactive and desireless) is no small accomplishment. This, indeed, is what our Lord asks of us through David: "Be still and know that I am God." This would be like saying: Learn to be empty of all things—interiorly and exteriorly—and you will behold that I am God.

St. John of the Cross
Ascent of Mt. Carmel

Those who meditate on Me with all their heart, who try to see Me in every creature, live in my love and security completely. I who am infinite, whom all the galaxies cannot contain, I live in such people, too.

Bhagavad Gita

The word "prayer" is full of religious overtones which are nearly as embarrassing as God. The trouble is that there *is*, as yet, no other word which does justice to the particular kind of attention I am trying to describe, the attention which Eastern Orthodox describe as "holding the mind in the heart." It isn't thinking, it isn't daydreaming, it isn't sleeping, it isn't talking, it isn't listening (at least when it works it isn't; in practice it easily slips into one or another of these things). It *is* a kind of tension, but a tension which can only come when there has been an inner relaxation, just as the Zen archer can only shoot his arrow correctly if his muscles are properly relaxed, so that they "look on impassively."

> Monica Furlong
> *Contemplating Now*

When the mind is still, tranquil, not seeking any answer or any solution, neither resisting nor avoiding—it is only then that there can be regeneration, because then the mind is capable of perceiving what is true; and it is truth that liberates, not your effort to be free.

J. Krisnamurti
Total Freedom

Weary spirit, go now to rest and forget all pictures, close your eyes softly; what is not God, let be forgotten, be quiet for the Lord and hold still for him, that he may enact in you what he wants.

Gerhard Tersteegen
Ein Leben in der Gegenwart Gottes

The mind is essentially a process, a flow of thoughts. The faster and more turbulent this flow is, the harder it is to go below the surface level of awareness into the unconscious realms where our desires and fears, problems and aspirations arise. In meditation, we teach the mind to go slowly with concentration through the words of a passage that embodies the highest of spiritual ideals. In this way we can gradually slow down the furious rush of thought, giving increasing self-mastery. Finally in the climax of meditation, we discover the real core of our personality, which the Hindu scriptures call simply *Atman*—our real self.

Eknath Easwaren
Dialogue with Death

I have spoken heretofore of emptiness, that is, of innocence, to the effect that the more innocent and poor the soul is, the less it has to do with creatures, the emptier of things that are not God, the more surely it takes to God, gets into him and is made One with him, itself becoming God. Then, to use St. Paul's words, the soul sees God face to face, and no longer as an idea or image.

Meister Eckhart

At the still point of the turning world.
Neither flesh nor fleshless;
Neither from nor towards;
At the still point, there the dance is,
But neither arrest nor movement.
And do not call it fixity,
Where past and future are gathered.
Neither movement from nor towards,
Neither ascent nor decline.
Except for the point, the still point,
There would be no dance,
And there is only the dance.
I can only say, *there* we have been:
But I cannot say where.
And I cannot say, how long,
For that is to place it in time.

T. S. Eliot
Four Quartets

Be still then, and know that I am God.

Psalm 46:10
Book of Common Prayer

6. *Attempts to Speak of Forgiveness*

Medical and psychological researchers have documented the positive effects of forgiveness on the forgiver. Forgiveness is related to lower risk for cardiovascular disease. It is said to be the key to long-term marriage. People with greater ability to forgive are happier, better adjusted, and more skillful in interpersonal relationships. Religious and spiritual leaders have advised forgiveness for thousands of years. In this regard, as in others, a physical and psychological truth is the foundation of an institutional religious tradition. Forgiveness, as Shakespeare's Portia told us in *The Merchant of Venice*, blesses both the giver and the recipient. This is true even when the giver of forgiveness and the recipient are the same person—yourself.

Be ye therefore merciful,
As your Father also is merciful.
Judge not, and ye shall not be judged:
Condemn not, and ye shall not be condemned:
forgive, and ye shall be forgiven.

Luke 6:36-37

Nothing worth doing is completed in our lifetime;
therefore, we are saved by hope. Nothing true or beautiful
or good makes complete sense in any immediate context
of history; therefore, we are saved by faith. Nothing we do,
however virtuous, can be accomplished alone; therefore
we are saved by love. No virtuous act is quite as virtuous
from the standpoint of our friend or foe as from our own;
therefore we are saved by the final form of love, which
is forgiveness.

> H. Richard Niebuhr
> *The Responsible Self*

It is freeing to become aware that we do not have to be victims of our past and can learn new ways of responding. But there is a step beyond this recognition . . . It is the step of forgiveness. Forgiveness is love practiced among people who love poorly. It sets us free without wanting anything in return.

Henri Nouwen
A Cry for Mercy

There is no condition for forgiveness.

Paul Tillich
The Courage to Be

It is one of the things about forgiveness you have to remember. It is not Spiritual. It is part of real politics.

Desmond Tutu
Reconcilation: The Ubuntu Theology of Desmond Tutu

Without being forgiven, released from the consequences of what we have done, our capacity to act would, as it were, be confined to a single deed from which we could never recover; we would remain the victims of its consequences forever, not unlike the sorcerer's apprentice, who lacked the magic formula to break the spell . . . Forgiveness is the key to action and freedom.

Hanna Arendt
The Human Condition

In this way you will be freed from the bondage of karma, and from its results both pleasant and painful. Then, with your heart free, you will come to Me.

Bhagavad Gita

All religions stress the power of forgiveness, and this power is never more deeply felt than when someone is dying. through forgiving and being forgiven, we purify ourselves of the darkness of what we have done, and prepare ourselves most completely for the journey through death.

Sogyal Rinpoche
The Tibetan Book of Living and Dying

If one by one we counted people out
For the least sin, it wouldn't take us long
To get so we had no one else to live with.
For to be social is to be forgiven.

Robert Frost
The Star-Splitter

It is in forgiving that we are forgiven.

Francis of Assisi

This is certain, that a man that studieth revenge keeps his wounds green, which otherwise would heal and do well.

Francis Bacon

The quality of mercy is not strain'd,
It droppeth as the gentle rain from heaven
Upon the place beneath: it is twice bless'd;
It blesseth him that gives and him that takes.

William Shakespeare
The Merchant of Venice

To be wronged is nothing unless you continue to
   remember it.

       Confucius

And forgive us our trespasses,
As we forgive those who trespass against us.

From The Lord's Prayer

7. Attempts to Speak of Humility

If you have been fortunate enough to know someone who is consistently humble, you have observed that such a person draws people to himself or herself. We all know of historical figures for whom this was true: Mahatma Ghandi, Mother Teresa, and others. But persons who are truly and consistently humble are rare. More commonly we see humble conduct temporarily expressed by ordinary, flawed people like ourselves.

Humility is not meekness. It is not self-abasement. It is the result of caring more for the welfare of others than for oneself. It is loving kindness in action. It is being a member of the team without needing to be the star.

Humility bestows enormous personal power because it reflects freedom from self-concern, and a person who is free from self-concern is fearless.

We do not presume to come to this thy Table,
O merciful Lord, trusting in our own righteousness,
But in thy manifold and great mercies.
We are not worthy so much
As to gather the crumbs under thy Table.

> Communion Service
> *Book of Common Prayer*

And whosoever shall exalt himself
Shall be abased;
And he that shall
Humble himself,
Shall be exalted.

Matthew 23:12

God resisteth the proud,
But giveth grace unto the humble.

James 4:6

He shall save the humble person.

Job 22:29

To one of the bretheren appeared a devil transformed into an angel of light, who said to him: "I am the angel Gabriel, and I have been sent to thee." But the brother said: "Think again, you must have been sent to someone else. I haven't done anything to deserve an angel." Immediately the devil ceased to appear.

Thomas Merton
The Wisdom of the Desert

Now therefore, after ascending all these steps of humility, the monk will quickly arrive at that perfect love of God that casts out fear.

The Rule of St. Benedict

All heavenly visions, revelations, and feelings—or whatever else one may desire to think on—are not worth as much as the least act of humility. Humility has the effects of charity: it neither esteems or seeks its own, it thinks no evil save of itself, it thinks no good of self but of others. Consequently souls should not look for their happiness in these supernatural apprehensions, but should strive to forget them for the sake of being free.

St. John of the Cross
Ascent of Mt. Carmel

I will briefly tell you of the eternal state all scriptures affirm, which can be entered only by those who are self controlled and free from selfish passions. Those who are selfless in their daily lives and free from selfish attachments attain this supreme goal.

Bhagavad Gita

This sense of poverty before Mystery is called humility, and to me this is the most important sign of an authentic religious experience. In the end, that humility is the best response to the view that religion is just a psychological phenomenon, the projection of infantile feelings of omnipotence. Humility shuns all power, respects the demands of justice and shares with all mortals the challenge of death.

Lorenzo Albacete
"A Very Fine Line"

It is humility that exalts one and favors him against
his friends.

Kenyan Proverb

Successful indeed are the believers
Who are humble in their prayers,
and who shun vain conversation,
and who are payers of the poor-due,
and who guard their modesty.

Qur'an

Be humble, be harmless, have no pretension, be upright, forbearing; serve your teacher in true obedience, keeping the mind and body in cleanness, tranquil, steadfast, master of ego, standing apart from the things of the senses, free from self; aware of the weakness in mortal nature.

Bhagavad Gita

Know the masculine but keep to the feminine,
Be the valley of the world.
Being the valley of the world,
He dwells in constant virtue,
He returns to the state of the newborn.

Know honor but keep to humility,
Be the riverbank of the universe.
Being the riverbank of the universe,
One finds contentment,
One returns to the state of the Uncarved Block.

Tao Te Ching

All men are children of Adam, and Adam was created from soil.

Hadith of Tirmidhi

Be of an exceedingly humble spirit, for the end of man is the worm.

Mishnah, *Abot*

Even if all the world tells you, "You are righteous," consider yourself wicked.

Talmud, *Nidda*

The fool who knows that he is a fool is for that very reason a wise man; the fool who thinks he is wise is called a fool indeed.

Dhammapada

Subhuti, what do you think? Does a holy one say within himself, "I have obtained Perfective Enlightenment"?

Subhuti replied, "No, World-honored One, if a holy one of Perfective Enlightenment said to himself, Such am I, he would necessarily partake of the idea of an ego-identity, a personality, a being, a separated individuality."

Diamond Sutra

The sage knows himself but makes no pretense.
He respects himself but is not proud.
He chooses what to keep and what to discard.

Tao Te Ching

Lord, what is man,
That thou hast
Such respect unto him:
Or the son of man,
That thou regardest him?
Man is like a thing of nought:
His time passeth away like a shadow.

Psalm 144:3-4
Book of Common Prayer

8. Attempts to Speak of Death

There is no line of demarcation separating us from the world. Flowing through us on a daily basis are the products of the earth and sky: our food, water, and the air we breathe. Also flowing through us are the ideas and feelings we give to and receive from those around us. We are expressions of the inexhaustible processes at work in the universe; in that sense, we are part of the eternal.

If we were truly able to "love our neighbors as ourselves," we would have no concern for death, because the lives of our neighbors would be equally important to us, and those lives continue after we are gone. But such an attitude is for saints and heroes. Instead, we more often think about ourselves and the legacy of our time on earth. Each of us asks: Do I have an immortal soul? Do I continue?

Perhaps the limitations of our minds is an indication of possibilities beyond our comprehension. Throughout the ages, men and women from every discipline and every walk of life have attempted to understand and communicate the nature of reality. But human ideas and the words used to convey them are not the Reality they seek to describe. This is as true of the mundane and everyday, as it is of the profound. My idea of a blade of grass is immeasurably different from complex processes at work in the living grass growing just outside my window. My concept of the universe is dwarfed by the incomprehensible fact that there is no limit to the night sky. My idea of reality is not Reality. My idea of God is not God.

If the nature of Reality is something more than we can put into words or mathematical formulas, if it transcends the limits of our minds, shouldn't we be comforted by the knowledge that we are part of an impenetrable and wonderful Mystery, whether we call it God or the Unknown, whether we attempt to approach it through the scientific method or prayer? It would seem reasonable, even inevitable, to be reassured by the understanding that there is, as William James said, "something More," something more to existence, something more to life and death than we can understand.

Before the mountains were brought forth,
Or ever the earth and the world were made:
Thou art God from everlasting,
And world without end.
Thou turnest man to destruction:
Again thou sayest,
Come again ye children of men.
For a thousand years in thy sight are but as yesterday:
Seeing that is past as a watch in the night.
As soon as thou scatterest them,
They are even as asleep:
And fade away suddenly like the grass.

Book of Common Prayer

Man that is born of woman hath but a short time to live,
And is full of misery,
He cometh up, and is cut down, like a flower;
He fleeth as it were a shadow,
And never continueth in one stay.
In the midst of life we are in death:
Of whom may we seek for succor,
But of thee, O Lord?

Book of Common Prayer

I am the daughter of Earth and Water.
And the nursling of the Sky;
I pass through the pores of the ocean and shores;
I change but I cannot die.

Percy Bysshe Shelley
The Cloud

"The everlasting nature of God, which in a sense is nontemporal and in another sense is temporal, may establish with the soul a peculiarly intense relationship of mutual immanence. Thus in some important sense the existence of the soul may be freed from its complete dependence upon the bodily organization."

Alfred North Whitehead
Adventures of Ideas

Nothing of him that doth fade,
But doth suffer a sea-change
Into something rich and strange.

William Shakespeare
The Tempest

Free from self-will, aggressiveness, arrogance, anger, and the lust to possess people or things, he is at peace with himself and with others, and enters into the unitive state. United with Brahman, ever joyful, beyond the reach of desire and sorrow, he has equal regard for every living creature and attains supreme devotion to Me. By loving Me he comes to know Me truly; then he knows my glory and enters into my boundless being. All his acts are performed in my service, and through my grace he wins eternal life.

Bhagavad Gita

Death is nothing to us, it matters not one jot, since the nature of the mind is understood to be mortal.

Lucretius
De Rerum Natura

The all-knowing Self was never born, nor will it die. Beyond cause and effect, this Self is eternal, immutable. When the body dies, the Self does not die. If the slayer believes that he can slay or the slain believes that he can be slain, neither knows the truth. The eternal Self slays not, nor is ever slain. Hidden in the heart of every creature exists the Self, subtler than the subtlest, greater than the greatest. They go beyond sorrow who extinguish their self will and behold the glory of the Self through the grace of the Lord of Love.

The Katha Upanishad
Dialogue with Death

Nothing in the world is single,
All things by a law divine
In one spirit meet and mingle.

> Percy Bysshe Shelley
> *Love's Philosophy*

Death is not an event in life; we do not live to experience death. Our life has no end in just the way in which our visual field has no limits.

Ludwig Wittgenstein and Bertrand Russell
Tractatus Logico-philosophicus

One's being or "personal identity" . . . is constituted by those experiences like honesty and courage which "characterize" a creature's continuing sequence of experiences. The creature forges its unique character by acting in a more or less consistent manner, yet at the same time the character so formed affects the creature's future actions and experiences. Being, in sum, is an abstract aspect of our becoming, not a thing in and of itself . . . Once the process of becoming is completed in death, all that we have achieved and experienced becomes a unified experience, our completed being. We exist in God eternally as this distinct being.

> J. Norman King and Barry L. Whitney
> "Rahner and Hartshorne on Death and Eternal Life"

It is becoming and not what has become which passes away. What perishes is not the secret extract of life, but the process of preparation. When this process, which we call life, has come to an end, then the perfect has arrived, and this is ourselves as we have become in freedom.

Karl Rahner

Our revels now are ended. These our actors,
As I fortold you, were all spirits and
Are melted into air, into thin air:
And, like the baseless fabric of this vision,
The cloud-capp'd towers, the gorgeous palaces,
The solemn temples, the great globe itself,
Yea, all which it inherit, shall dissolve
And, like this insubstantial pageant faded,
Leave not a rack behind. We are such stuff
As dreams were made of, and our little life
Is rounded with a sleep.

William Shakespeare
The Tempest

Time, like an ever-rolling stream
Bears all our years away;
They fly, forgotten, as a dream
Dies at the opening day.
O God, our help in ages past,
Our hope for years to come,
Be thou our guide while life shall last
And our eternal home.

Isaac Watts
"O God, our help in ages past"
(This hymn paraphrases Psalm 90:1-5)

Can I live with death? Which means that everything I have done and collected ends? Ending is more important than continuity. The ending means the beginning of something new. If you merely continue, it is the same pattern being repeated in a different mold. So can I live with death? That means freedom, complete, total, holistic freedom. And in that freedom there is great love and compassion, and that intelligence which is not an end, which is immense.

J. Krishnamurti
Total Freedom

When the human being "listens to itself," in depth, it . . . discovers that the "I" to which we attribute all our acts does not possess sufficient consistency to be the ultimate foundation of these acts . . . persons discover that, in their deepest heart, there is a "bottomless bottom," that "is" what they largely are, and at the same time is identical to what each "other" human can likewise experience—the bottom that constitutes what is deepest in every human being, as anyone who has had this experience can attest—the same depth, moreover, that is lived, perceived, intuited as the unique source of all things, and yet never exhausted in any of them . . . the experience of the ultimate, constitutive reality of each being: "there is" an ultimate "something," at once immanent and transcendent, that is what we really "are." This "something" is not distinct from me: it is my deepest I.

Raimundo Panikkar
The Silence of God

Must we ourselves live on consciously forever to render our present lives meaningful? Hartshorne cautions against such an egocentric self-interest, a view that he sees as explicitly denying that we can genuinely love either God or one another . . . Whatever good we accomplished in our earthly lives will be used by God in an endless variety of new perspectives. As such, our lives, while consciously completed, contribute everlastingly to God.

> J. Norman King and Barry L. Whitney
> "Rahner and Hartshorne on Death and Eternal Life"

As we gaze into the void of our future extinguished self and dissolving substance, we encounter there the wellspring of life and creativity from which all things have sprung and into which they return, only to well up again in new forms . . . Then, like bread tossed on water, we can be confident that our creative work will be nourishing to the community of life, even as we relinquish our small self back into the great Self.

Rosemary Radford Ruether
Gaia and God

For as in Adam all die:
Even so in Christ
Shall all be made alive.

1 Corinthians 15:22

Behold I shew you a mystery:
We shall not all sleep,
But we shall all be changed.
For this corruptible must put on incorruption,
And this mortal must put on immortality;
Then shall be brought to pass the saying that is written,
Death is swallowed up in victory.
O death, where is thy sting?
O grave, where is thy victory?

Book of Common Prayer

Notes

1. Roger S. Jones, *Physics as Metaphor.* Minneapolis, Minn.: University of Minnesota Press, 1990, p. 241.

2. Abraham Joshua Heschel, *God in Search of Man: A Philosophy of Judaism.* New York: Noonday Press, 1997, pp.122-123.

3. Raimundo Panikkar, *Invisible Harmony: Essay on Contemplation and Responsibility.* Minneapolis, Minn.: Fortress Press, 1995, p. 101.

4. Friedrich Wilhelm Nietzsche, *Thus Spake Zarathustra.* Translated by Thomas Common. Amherst, N.Y.: Prometheus Books: 1993, Chapter 2.

5. W. MacNeile Dixon, *The Human Situation.* New York: Gordon Press, 1973.

Acknowledgments

Lorenzo Albacete, "A Very Fine Line," *The New York Times Magazine,* 17 December, 2000. Reprinted by permission from the author.

Annie Besant, Prayer 902, "O Hidden Life, vibrant in every atom" from *The Oxford Book of Prayer,* edited by George Appleton (1985). Used by permission.

Matthew E. Bunson, from *The Wisdom Teachings of the Dalai Lama* by Matthew E. Bunson, copyright © 1997 by Matthew E. Bunson. Used by permission of Dutton, a division of Penguin Putnam, Inc.

E. E. Cummings, excerpt from "i thank You God for this most amazing day." Copyright 1950, © 1978, 1991 by the Trustees for the E. E. Cummings Trust. Copyright © 1979 by George James Firmage, from *Complete Poems: 1904–1962* by E. E. Cummings, edited by George J. Firmage. Used by permission of Liveright Publishing Corporation.

Annie Dillard, from "Holy Sparks: A Prayer for the Silent God," *Notre Dame Magazine,* Winter, 1998–1999. Reprinted by permission from Russell & Volkening as agents for the author. Copyright © 1975 by Annie Dillard.

Eknath Easwaran, excerpts from *The Dhammapada*, translated by Eknath Easwaran, founder of the Blue Mountain Center of Meditation, copyright © 1985; reprinted by permission of Nilgiri Press, Tomales, Calif., *www.nilgiri.org*. Also reprinted by permission of Nilgiri Press were excerpts from the following books written by Easwaran: *Dialogue with Death,* copyright © 1981 and *Like a Thousand Suns,* copyright © 1979.

T. S. Eliot, an extract from "Burnt Norton," *Four Quartets, Section II,* from *Collected Poems, 1909–1962* by T. S. Eliot, published by Faber & Faber Ltd. Used with permission.

Robert Frost, excerpt from "The Star-Splitter" by Robert Frost from *The Poetry of Robert Frost.* Edited by Edward Connery Lathem. Copyright 1923, © 1969 by Henry Holt & Co., copyright 1951 by Robert Frost. Reprinted by permission of Henry Holt and Company, LLC.

Abraham Joshua Heschel, excerpts from *God in Search of Man* by Abraham Joshua Heschel. Copyright © 1955 by Abraham Joshua Heschel. Copyright renewed © 1983 by Sylvia Heschel. Reprinted by permission of Farrar, Straus and Giroux, LLC.

Roger S. Jones, excerpts from pp. 220, 224 in *Physics as Metaphor* by Roger S. Jones. University of Minnesota Press, 1990. Used by permission from the author.

J. Norman King and Barry L. Whitney, excerpts from "Rahner and Hartshorne on Death and Eternal Life" in *Horizons,* vol. 15, Fall 1988. Reprinted by permission of the authors.

J. Krishnamurti, excerpts from *Total Freedom: the Essential Krishnamurti,* copyright © 1996 by Krishnamurti Foundation of America and

Selected Bibliography

Albacete, Lorenzo. "A Very Fine Line." *New York Times Magazine,* 17 Dec., 2000.

Arendt, Hannah, and Margaret Canovan. *The Human Condition*. Chicago: University of Chicago Press, 1998.

Battle, Michael Jesse, and Desmond Mpilo Tutu. *Reconciliation: The Ubuntu Theology of Desmond Tutu*. Cleveland: Pilgrim Press, 1997.

Becker, Ernest, and Daniel P. Goleman. *The Denial of Death*. New York: Free Press, 1997.

Book of Common Prayer (1662). New York: Cambridge University Press, 1997.

Bunson, Matthew E., Dalai Lama, and Dalai Lama Bstan-dzin-rgya-mtsho. *The Wisdom Teachings of the Dalai Lama*. New York: Plume, 1997.

Candrakirti. *Prasannapada*. Boulder, Colo.: Prajn Press, 1979.

Carus, Titus Lucretius. *Nature of Things*. Translated by Frank O. Copley. New York: W. W. Norton, 1977.

Cooper, David A. *God Is a Verb: Kabbalah and the Practice of Mystical Judaism*. New York: Penguin, 1998.

Cummings, E. E. *Complete Poems. 1904–1962*. Edited by George James Firmage. New York: Liveright, 1979.

The Dhammapada. Translated by Eknath Easwaran. Introduced by Stephen Ruppenthal. Tomales, Calif.: Nilgiri Press, 1986.

De Mello, Anthony. *The Way to Love: The Last Meditations of Anthony De Mello*. Bennington, Vt.: Image Books, 1995.

Dillard, Annie. *Holy the Firm*. New York: HarperCollins, 1999.

———. "Holy Sparks: A Prayer for the Silent God." *Notre Dame Magazine,* Winter 1998–99.

Dionysius the Areopagite, Bishop of Athens. *Letter to Gaius Therapeutes.*

Dixon, William MacNeile. *The Human Situation*. New York: Gordon Press, 1973.

Easwaran, Eknath. *Dialogue with Death: A Journey Through Consciousness*. Tomales, Calif.: Nilgiri Press, 1992.

———. *Like a Thousand Suns (The Bhagavad Gita for Daily Living)*. Tomales, Calif.: Nilgiri Press, 1979.

Eckhart, Meister, et. al. *Meister Eckhart: A Modern Translation*. Translated by Raymond B. Blakney. New York: HarperTorch, 1995.

Eliot, T. S. *Four Quartets*. San Diego, Calif.: Harvest Books, 1974.

Feynman, Richard Phillips. *The Meaning of It All: Thoughts of a Citizen Scientist*. New York: Longman Publishing, 1999.

Frost, Robert. *The Poetry of Robert Frost*. Edited by Edward Connery Lathem. New York: Henry Holt, 1951.

Furlong, Monica. *Contemplating Now*. Cambridge, Mass.: Cowley Publications, 1983.

Hartshorne, Charles. *Whitehead's Philosophy: Selected Essays, 1935–1970*. Lincoln, Neb.: University of Nebraska Press, 1972.

Heschel, Abraham Joshua. *God in Search of Man: A Philosophy of Judaism*. New York: Farrar, Straus & Giroux, 1997.

———. *Man's Quest for God*. New York: Aurora Press, 1998.

Hoffman, Banesh, and Helen Dukas. *Albert Einstein: Creator and Rebel*. New York: New American Library, 1989.

St. John of the Cross. *The Collected Works of Saint St. John of the Cross.* Translated by Kiernan Kavanaugh and Otilio Rodriguez. Washington, D.C.: Institute of Carmelite Studies, ICS Publications, 1991.

Jones, Roger S. *Physics as Metaphor.* Minneapolis, Minn.: University of Minnesota Press, 1990.

King, J. Norman and Barry L. Whitney, "Rahner and Hartshorne on Death and Eternal Life." *Horizons,* vol. 15, Fall, 1988.

Krishnamurti, J. *Total Freedom: The Essential Krishnamurti.* San Francisco: HarperSanFrancisco, 1996.

L'Engle, Madeleine. *Walking on Water: Reflections on Faith and Art.* New York: Random House, 1998.

Marechal, Joseph. *Etudes sur le Psycologie de Mystiques I.* Paris: Desclee, 1938.

Matt, Daniel Chanan. *The Essential Kabbalah: The Heart of Jewish Mysticism.* San Francisco: HarperSanFrancisco, 1995.

Matteo, Anthony M. "Can Belief in God Be Basic?" *Horizons,* vol. 15.

Mbiti, John S. *The Prayers of African Religion.* Maryknoll, N.Y.: Orbis Books, 1975.

Merton, Thomas. *The Wisdom of the Desert.* New York: W. W. Norton, 1988.

_____. *Zen and the Birds of Appetite.* New York: W. W. Norton, 1988.

Niebuhr, H. Richard. *The Responsible Self: An Essay in Christian Moral Philosophy.* Louisville, Ken.: Westminster John Knox Press, 1999.

Nietzsche, Friedrich Wilhelm. *Thus Spake Zarathustra.* Translated by Thomas Common. Amherst, N. Y.: Prometheus Books, 1993.

Nouwen, Henri J. M. *A Cry for Mercy: Prayers from the Genessee.* Maryknoll, N. Y.: Orbis Books, 1994.

The Oxford Book of Prayer. Edited by George Appleton. New York: Oxford University Press, 1985.

Panikkar, Raimundo, *Cosmotheandric Experience: Emerging Religious Consciousness.* Maryknoll, N. Y.: Orbis Books, 1993.

———. *Invisible Harmony: Essays on Contemplation and Responsibility.* Edited by Harry James Cargas. Minneapolis, Minn.: Fortress Press, 1995.

———. *The Silence of God: The Answer of the Buddha.* Maryknoll, New York: Orbis Books, 1989.

Rahner, Karl. *Foundations of Christian Faith: An Introduction to the Idea of Christianity.* New York: Crossroad, 1993.

Reuther, Rosemary Radford. *Gaia & God: An Ecofeminist Theology of Earth Healing.* San Francisco: HarperSanFrancisco, 1994.

Rinpoche, Sogyal. *The Tibetan Book of Living and Dying.* San Francisco: HarperSanFrancisco, 1994.

The Rule of St. Benedict: In English. Edited by Timothy Fry. Introduction by Thomas More. New York: Vintage Books, 1998.

Rumi, Jalal Al-Din. *The Essential Rumi.* Translated by Coleman Barks, et. al. New York: HarperCollins, 1997.

Shelley, Percy Bysshe. *Love's Philosophy.* New York: Dial Books, 1992.

Spong, John Shelby. *Why Christianity Must Change or Die: A Bishop Speaks to Believers in Exile.* San Francisco: HarperSanFrancisco, 1999.

———. *Resurrection: Myth or Reality?* San Francisco: HarperSanFrancisco, 1995.

St. Teresa of Avila. *The Way of Perfection.* Edited by Henry L. Carrigan. Orleans, Mass.: Paraclete Press, 2000.

Tersteegen, Gerhard. *Ein Leben in der Gegenwart Gottes.* Giessen & Basel: Brunnen-Verlag, 1960.

Tillich, Peter. *The Courage to Be*. Introduction by Peter J. Gomes. New Haven, Conn.: Yale University Press, 2000.

Tillich, Paul, *Systematic Theology*. Chicago: University of Chicago Press, 1967.

Whitehead, Alfred North. *Adventures of Ideas*. New York: Macmillan, 1967.

———. *Modes of Thought*. New York: Free Press, 1985.

———, and Donald W. Sherburne. *Process and Reality*. New York: Free Press, 1985.

Wittgenstein, Ludwig. *Philosophical Investigations/Philosophische Untersuchungen*. Translated by G. E. M. Anscombe. Williston, Vt.: American International Distribution Corp., 1998.

———, and Bertrand Arthur Russell. *Tractatus Logico-philosophicus*. New York: Routledge, Kegan & Paul, 1995.

Wotton, Henry. *The Character of a Happy Life*. 1614.